The History of Finland

A Fascinating Guide to this Nordic Country

By

Christopher Hughes

TABLE OF CONTENTS

Located in northern Europe, geographically Finland is one of the most northern, as well as most remote, countries in the world. Approximately one-third of its territory lies north of the Arctic Circle. Finland is also relatively young, recently celebrating only its 100th anniversary. Of particular significance, the country forms the very symbolic and historic northern border between western and eastern Europe.

It was not until after the Russian Revolution that Finland declared its independence—on December 6, 1917—and the country was formed. Prior to that, from 1809-1917, the geographical area that is now Finland was a Russian territory. And prior to that, it was a territory of Sweden. The earliest written mentioning of Finland is from the 12th century.

For ease of reference in this article, the term "Finland" will be used to refer to the territories that ultimately became the country of Finland, both before and after.

ANCIENT FINLAND

Because there is no written record of Finland until the 12th century, very little is known about its earliest human settlement. It is believed that the first permanent inhabitants arrived 10,000 to 12,000 years ago as the glaciers receded at the end of the last Ice Age. But it most certainly was inhabited long before then. Flint tools found in a cave at Kristinestad suggest a human presence much farther back, between Ice Ages.

As would be expected from its geographical location, the first settlers came from Russia and the area of present-day Estonia. Ancient sites of inhabitation have been found in southern Finland believed to date back to the eighth millennium B.C. A Roman historian mentioned a tribe called the "Fenni" in the first century A.D. He essentially described the tribe members as "wild savages" who did not have homes or horses.

Many people mistakenly assume that the Finns took part in the Viking expeditions during the Viking Age (c. 800 - 1050). They did not. The confusion most likely arises from much of the world's incorrect use of the terms "Scandinavian" and "Nordic" interchangeably. Iceland, Norway, Sweden, Finland, and Denmark are all Nordic countries with Scandinavian roots. But in northern Europe, only Norwegian, Swedish, and Danish people refer to themselves as "Scandinavian."

The Nordic countries with historical connections to the Vikings are Sweden, Denmark, Iceland, and Norway. Because of the misplaced collective use of "Scandinavian," many people lump Finland in there with the Vikings as well. Finnish people, the majority of whom live in Finland (the rest primarily in Sweden) are also one of the Nordic peoples. They fall into the Uralic people, a mixed race of Mongoloid and Europoid, with no relationship to the Vikings.

The Swedish Period (12th Century – 1809)

Prior to the middle of the 12th century, Finland essentially was a political and religious non-entity. During the Viking Age, Swedish Vikings engaged in eastward expeditions aimed at establishing trade ties with the Arab world via Russia. Although the Swedes then came into contact with the Finns, they did not build any permanent settlements there during that time.

Towards the close of the Viking Age, Swedish influence in Finland grew. The Roman Catholic Church had been successful converting most Swedes to Christianity, and during the wave of the crusades that began in 1095, most Finns ultimately were converted as well.

The Swedish Crusades (1155-1323)

Although accounts vary, semi-historical legend maintains that King Erik IX led the First Swedish Crusade in Finland in 1155. He is credited with conquering southwest Finland for his country. It appeared, however, that Christianity did not yet have a stronghold there at that time. Interestingly, Pope Alexander III wrote a letter to one of the Swedish archbishops in the late 1100s, stating: "The Finns always promise to obey the Christian faith whenever they are threatened by a hostile army … but when the army retires, they deny the faith, despise the preachers, and grievously persecute them."

In 1249, Birger Jarl led the Second Swedish Crusade, bringing the central region of Finland under Swedish control. And then in the late 1200s and early 1300s, the Third Swedish Crusade, aimed directly at the already Christianized Karelia region in Novgorod (Russia), conquered that area for Sweden as well. In 1323, the Treaty of Pähkinäsaari drew the boundary between Russian and Swedish control. With Finland now firmly part of the Swedish realm, the crusades were ended.

* * *

It was not until 1362 that Finns began to enjoy the equal status of Swedes, including the right to participate in royal elections. But even prior to that time, the Swedes had begun to treat Finland as "their own." As to be expected, the social and legal systems of Sweden infiltrated Finland, but this did not include feudalism. The Finnish peasants always maintained their personal freedom, never being subjected to serfdom. This is not to say that the farmers possessed much political power, though, which was relegated primarily to Swedish-speaking nobility.

Finland enjoyed a period of prosperity, growth, and economic development during the 15th and 16th centuries. In 1521, Gustav Vasa became the King of Sweden, and during his rule and in large part as a result of his efforts, the Swedish church was reformed. Martin Luther had initiated the Protestant Reformation in Germany, and Scandinavian countries had historically been receptive to German influence. Thus, Lutheranism spread quickly, and by the time Luther died in 1546, it was firmly implanted in Scandinavia, including Sweden, and thus Finland.

King Vasa's motivation in regard to this conversion undoubtedly was based largely upon his desire for a stronger centralized state; the acceptance of Lutheranism enabled him to break the political power of the Roman Catholic Church, which had previously stood in his way. Prior to the Reformation, the Church had owned about one-fifth of the land in Sweden. Therefore, the ensuing confiscation of Church properties resulted in a huge windfall for the monarchy as well as the aristocracy.

In 1550, Helsinki was founded by King Vasa (then under the name of "Helsingfors"), but it was essentially only a fishing village for more than two centuries before becoming Finland's capital in 1812. It was around this time—the mid-1500s—that the Bishop of Turku, Mikael Agricola, published the Finnish translation of the New Testament, the first appearance of Finnish in print. Therefore, Agricola is considered to be the "father" of the Finnish literary language. He had studied under Luther and recognized the tremendous importance of the translation of the Bible, and later translated parts of the Old Testament and wrote other religious works as well. There can be no question that literacy in Finland—specifically in Finnish—was increased as a result of the Reformation's emphasis on religious instruction in the vernacular languages.

While King Vasa managed to avoid Sweden's involvement in foreign wars, his successors sought to expand the power he had established. Their aggressive foreign policy brought Sweden into direct conflict with Russia, Poland, and Denmark, all of which had an interest in the Baltic, as of course did Sweden. What resulted was a warlike era beginning in the late-16th century that lasted for many years.

The Cudgel (or Club) War (1596-1597)

During the late 1500s, the Finns had been subjected to high taxes, drafts, and abuse by military personnel, and Finland itself was often exposed to Swedish military campaigns causing devastation to their countryside and people. When the peasants finally rebelled, the Cudgel War ensued.

The peasants' use of clubs as weapons is the root of the alternative name of "the Club War" for this conflict. Armed with clubs and various other blunt weapons, the peasants won a number of skirmishes, but ultimately were no match for the heavily armed and well-trained troops of Finnish (Swedish) Governor Klaus Fleming. A treaty was negotiated that required the surrender of peasant leader Jaakko Ilkka, but when Ilka fled, the peasants did as well.

Over the next two months, at least 1,500 peasants were killed, and on January 27, 1597, Ilkka and five other rebellion leaders were executed. Without a leader, the peasants still attempted to continue the rebellion and attacked Fleming on February 24, 1597. This time more than 1,000 peasants were killed and half as many again were captured. This marked the end of a bloody and brutal Cudgel War.

THE THIRTY YEARS' WAR (1618-1648)

At the start of the 17th century, Sweden was ruled by King Gustavus Adolphus (a.k.a. King Gustav II Adolf), i.e., 1611-1632. He successfully transformed the Swedish army from a peasant militia into perhaps the most powerful army in all of Europe at the time. Sweden's conquest of Livonia had been completed, and pursuant to the Treaty of Stolbova, more territories were gained from a divided Russia.

In 1630, King Adolphus decided to intervene in the already raging Thirty Years' War that had begun in 1618 as a struggle between Catholic and Protestant factions in Germany. Taking the side of the northern Protestants, the Swedish (and Finnish) armies invaded Central Europe, and their involvement represented a major turning point in the war. Previously on the verge of defeat, the Protestant cause won several major victories.

It was during the Thirty Years' War that the Finnish cavalry, the "Hakkapeliittas" or "Hackapells," earned their reputation, specifically as being both brave and brutal. Their name was derived from their famous cry: "*Hakkaa paalle*!" meaning "Hack them down!" Upon King Adolphus's entry into the war, and specifically his campaign in Germany, he was joined by twelve mighty companies of Hakkapeliitas.

Compared to their German counterparts, the Finnish horses of the Hakkapeliitas were small … so small that it was reported that the Imperial Army commander, Count Johan de Tilly, actually laughed at the sight of them on the battlefield at Breitenfeld in 1631. He grossly underestimated these soldiers and their quick and highly maneuverable horses. The Hakkapelitas' formidable capabilities were firmly established both at the Battle of Breitenfeld as well as others. There is no question that the prowess of these Finnish horsemen in the Thirty Years' War contributed to the rise of Sweden as a major power, both during this war and after.

With more than eight million casualties resulting from battles, famine, and disease, the Thirty Years' War remains one of the most brutal wars in human history. Swedish King Adolphus was one such casualty, killed in 1932 in the Battle of Lützen.

It was reputed that Gustavus's habit was to enter battle wearing no armor, proclaiming, "The Lord God is my armor!" Historians consider that it is more likely that he simply wore a leather cuirass (a piece of armor made from metal or other rigid material, in this case leather, which covers the torso with both a chest- or breastplate and a back plate). In 1627, a Polish soldier had shot Gustavus in the muscles above the shoulders, but the doctors couldn't remove the bullet and two fingers on his right hand were paralyzed; it was reported that from that point forward, the king could not wear iron armor.

The Battle of Lützen on November 6, 1632 was one of the most decisive battles of the Thirty Years' War. In the thick fog and gun smoke of battle, King Gustavus was separated from his fellow riders, and both he and his horse suffered gunshots—the king to his left arm and the horse to the neck. With his horse difficult to control, and in the increasing smoke from the burning town of Lützen, Gustavus inadvertently ended up behind enemy lines where he was again shot, this time in the back, and then stabbed. While lying on the ground, a final—and fatal—shot to the temple was administered. Although the Battle of Lützen was considered to be a Protestant victory, the Protestant alliance lost one of its most valued leaders.

Several significant reforms were made in Finland during the Thirty Years' War. In 1640, Finland's first university, the Royal Academy of Abo, was founded in Turku. Further, in 1642, the entire Bible was published in Finnish. By contrast, though, the continuing wars, as well as the cold climate (later to become known as "the Little Ice Age") and high taxation, made this era in Sweden quite oppressive for Finnish peasants.

The Thirty Years' War lost its religious character after 1635, becoming almost purely political. After battles occurring over most of Europe for three decades, the war finally ended in 1648 with the Treaty of Westphalia. And with it, the balance of power and map of Europe had been radically, and in some ways irrevocably, changed. The member states of the Holy Roman Empire were granted full sovereignty. Spain had lost both the Netherlands (which was recognized as an independent republic), as well as its prior dominant position in Western Europe. France had now moved into the position of the chief Western power. And a modern Europe with a community of sovereign states was established.

* * *

The 17th century in Finland was also marked by a period of extremely strict Lutheran orthodoxy. Church attendance was mandatory, and every subject was required to confess the Lutheran faith. Further, each person had to possess a level of literacy sufficient to read the Bible, resulting in the tremendous benefit of widespread education.

In the late 1600s, Finland was absolutely decimated by a famine, known as the Great Famine of 1695-1697, or simply "the Great Famine." It swept through Estonia, Finland, Latvia, Norway, and Sweden, but Finland was definitely one of the worst affected areas. In just two years, approximately a third of the Finnish population was wiped out, i.e., about 150,000 people.

THE GREAT NORTHERN WAR (1700-1721)

In 1697, Sweden crowned Charles XII, then only fifteen years old, and Sweden's rivals viewed Charles' youth as a weakness for his country. One such rival was Swedish monarch, Peter the Great. He had been a friend of the Swedish monarchy until 1699, but took advantage of an opportunity to join an alliance with King Augustus of Poland and King Frederick IV of Denmark (the latter of whom was Charles XII's cousin). Thus began another age-old story—kings warring over territory.

The alliance against Sweden was quickly surprised by the young King Charles' military abilities. He summarily knocked Denmark out of the war in 1700 and then Poland in 1706. Now overly confident, King Charles marched on Moscow in the summer of 1709, but was defeated handily at the Battle of Poltava. Between casualties and prisoners, the Swedes lost as many as 20,000 troops, and days later most of the remainder of their army surrendered to the Russians.

Denmark and Poland then rejoined their efforts with Russia, and the Great Northern War continued on until 1721. Pursuant to the Treaty of Nystad ending the war, Sweden had to cede the southeastern part of Finland to Russia, along with Ingria, Estonia, and Livonia. In addition, Sweden was forced to pay a large indemnity to Russia, but in exchange, the Russians evacuated Finland.

The Russo-Swedish War / Hats' War (1741-1743)

Just a few short years later, the Russians and Swedes were right back at war again over Finland. A Swedish political party known as "the Hats" was credited with the instigation of what became known as "the Hats' War" in an attempt to regain the portions of Finland lost to Russia during the Great Northern War.

The original plan was for Swedish forces to invade St. Petersburg (then known as Petrograd) in Russia, setting up the overthrow of the government. The Swedes boldly declared war in late July 1741, but the planned first attack was delayed as a result of an epidemic among the Swedish fleet along Russian borders. With the death of many Swedish troops, Russia took full advantage and attacked, winning the first battle.

Unfortunately for the Finns, most of this Russo-Swedish war ended up being fought in Finland. For three years, the war mostly consisted of the Russians attacking and the Swedes defending. Although the Russians overall won this war, as part of the negotiations, the Empress of Russia, Elizabeth, offered to give back to Sweden more areas of Finland if her heir's uncle, Adolf Frederick of Holstein-Gottorp, would be named successor to the Swedish throne. Believing this would ultimately benefit Sweden, the Hats agreed, and the Empress instructed her forces to leave Finland.

With the signing of the Treaty of Abo (a.k.a. the Treaty of Turku) in August 1743, the Hats' War ended. Some relevant portions of that treaty included that:

- There was to be "an eternal peace and perfect friendship" between the two warring countries, i.e., Russia and Sweden.
- Hostilities from either / both sides were to cease immediately.
- Sweden was to consent to declare his Highness the Prince Adolph Frederick as successor to the Swedish crown.
- Boundaries were designated as to territories that Sweden yielded to Russia and vice versa.

- In the event of a threatened attack of Sweden, Russia would take necessary measures to prevent the same.

THE RUSSIAN PERIOD (1809-1917)

After almost 500 years of Swedish sovereignty, in 1809 the "Russian Period" in Finland officially began. During the Napoleonic wars, France and Russia had become allies, and Napoleon urged Tsar Alexander I of Russia to force Sweden into joining them against Britain. The Tsar obliged and in 1808 invaded a weak and poorly organized (Swedish) Finland. Earlier Swedish strategic directives (from 1785) referenced that in the event of a Russian attack of Finland, Swedish forces should withdraw, and further, in the event of "extreme danger," all of Finland should be evacuated. This is exactly what occurred in 1808. Pursuant to the Treaty of Hamina, Finland was formally ceded to Russia by Sweden on September 17, 1809.

In Porvoo, a city at the mouth of the Porvoo River on the Gulf of Finland, the political framework of Finland under Russian power was formally established by the Diet of Porvoo ("diet" meaning legislative assembly) in 1809. Previously just a group of provinces, this was the first time that Finland as a whole became a united political entity. Thanks to the enlightened Russian emperor, Alexander I, Finland was given extensive autonomy. As a Grand Duchy (a territory ruled by a grand duke or duchess), Alexander I served as Finland's Grand Duke, and his representative in Finland was the Governor General.

Alexander promised to afford respect to the Finnish people, specifically in regard to their religion and fundamental privileges and laws. They were allowed to keep their constitution (from the Swedish era), their religion (Christianity), and the rights of their estates. From 1809 to 1863, the Governor General representing the Russian emperor was at times even a Finn. Further, the highest governing body in Finland was the Senate, whose members were Finns.

In 1812, the capital of Finland was moved from Turku to Helsinki, and a few years later the university (the Royal Academy of Abo) was moved from Turku to Helsinki as well. This became the now world-renowned University of Helsinki, which has been ranked as one of the top 100 universities in the world.

Generally, the Russian Period (also known as Finland's "era of bureaucracy") was a prosperous period for most Finns with minimal warfare and increasing growth. Due to such a vast rural and agrarian population, however, the dissemination of liberal and national ideas was greatly restricted. This issue became even more problematic when in 1850 an ordinance prohibited the publication of books in Finnish, the only exceptions being those intended for economic benefit or religious edification. Keep in mind that the majority of the population at that time only understood Finnish; a minimal one-seventh of the Finnish population spoke Swedish as their first language. Yet, Swedish was almost exclusively used in teaching at all levels (secondary and university) and it was the only language permitted within the Finnish administration. As one can imagine, this ordinance appeared to be clearly designed to maintain class distinctions in Finland.

Nevertheless, advocates of a Finnish-speaking Finland, known as "Fennomans," began to make strides. In 1858, the first purely Finnish-speaking grammar school was established. And just a few years later (1863), Alexander II issued The Language Decree pursuant to which Finnish actually became an official language; after a twenty-year transition period, Finnish was to be placed on an equal footing with Swedish in government and the courts.

Other reforms were had in Finland during the reign of Alexander II. Perhaps the most significant was his re-convening of the Diet in 1863 (the first since 1809), and then in 1869, the promulgation of the Diet ordinance providing that it should be convened regularly. From then on, there was active legislative work in Finland with the Diet meeting regularly. In 1865, Finland adopted its own monetary system (the markka). And the Conscription Act of 1878 established Finland's own army.

THE ERA OF FIRST OPPRESSION (1899-1905)

Prior to the end of Alexander II's reign, rumblings had begun in Russia to abolish Finnish autonomy. Fortunately for Finland, his successor, Alexander III, also resisted the movement of Russian nationalists to bring Finland into the Russian nation. But because Alexander I had exercised his supreme powers to grant Finland autonomous rights, in 1899 Emperor Nicholas II took the position that he was entitled to take them back. He issued a manifesto setting out his authority to enact laws enforceable in Finland if they affected Russian interests, even if without the Finnish Diet's consent.

This attempt at the destruction of Finnish separatism became known as "Russification."

In 1900, the imposition of Russian as Finland's third official language was ordered. The very next year it was decreed that Finland's army be disbanded and Finns would serve in the Russian military. Two opposing factions quickly formed within Finland politics: the Constitutionalists, who had no intention of observing what they considered to be illegal enactments; and the Compliers (or the "Old Finnish Party"), who would acquiesce to the Russians as long as it did not "affect Finland's vital interests." As to be expected, any Constitutionalists in office were immediately dismissed and exiled.

It was against this backdrop that Governor-General Nikolai Bobrikov was assassinated in 1904. After becoming the Governor-General in 1898, his Russification policies quickly made him unpopular in Finland. When Emperor Nicholas II granted him dictatorial power in 1903, Bobrikov gradually became a hated tyrant in the eyes of the Finns.

Eugen Schauman, a twenty-nine-year-old activist, who also happened to be the Junior Chief Accountant of the Supreme Board of Education, took upon himself the task of eliminating Bobrikov and his oppression from Finland. He also felt that the murder of Bobrikov would send a message to the Emperor as to the Finns' absolute discontent with Russification. Prior to executing his plan, Schauman wrote Emperor Nicholas a letter, taking full responsibility for his actions and apologizing beforehand, but also asking the tsar to take action in regard to what was going on in Finland, Poland, and the Baltic states.

On June 16, 1904, in the Senate building in Helsinki, Schauman shot Bobrikov three times before fatally turning the gun on himself. The Governor-General did not die immediately but did shortly thereafter from his injuries. Schauman's letter to the Emperor was found in his (Schauman's) pocket.

Because Bobrikov had become a symbol of the evil and repressive Russification in the empire, most Finns celebrated his death. And Schauman quickly became deemed a national hero who stood up for the entire Finnish population against Russification. The majority considered the assassination to be "righteous," particularly because Schauman had killed himself to atone for his bad deed. At the scene of the assassination (now the Government Palace) is a Schauman memorial plaque that says in Latin: *Se Pro Patria Dedit* (Given himself on behalf of fatherland).

Strangely, Tsar Nicholas II's response to the murder of his Governor-General was pretty much indifferent. The day after the assassination, the tsar wrote the following in his diary:

> *In the morning I got to know, to my sorrow, that Bobrikov died to his wounds at one o'clock in the night. The weather was warm. After the presentation I received 86 officers of the Nikolayev General Staff Academy in the halls, and after the breakfast, the Spanish emissary. Uncle Vladimir*

drank tea with us. I read a lot. I bicycled, and I shot two ravens, one yesterday. We ate dinner at the terrace. In the evening it was cooler.

* * *

The 1905 Russian Revolution, a period of tremendous unrest for Russia, gave Finland a period of relative peace. The Social Democratic Party (previously the Labor Party) began to develop along revolutionary lines, and was not willing to compromise with tsarist Russia. They (the Social Democrats) joined forces with the Constitutionalists to organize a national strike in 1905, forcing the Russian emperor to restore Finland's autonomy. As part of this effort, Finland's Parliamentary system was completely reformed as well—one of the Social Democrats' main objectives.

In 1906, Finland's political system was amazingly transformed from one of Europe's most unrepresentative to the most modern: a Parliamentary system based on universal suffrage (the right to vote). The political factions were polarized and the foundation for the modern party system was laid.

Notably, Finland was the first European country to recognize women's right to vote. With suffrage for all Finnish citizens aged twenty-four and up regardless of gender or social status, the farmers and working class potentially garnered a great majority. But the significance of Parliament was trivialized by the Russian Emperor's constant dissolution of it. Ultimately both the

Constitutionalists and even the Compliers resigned from the government, deflated and defeated. A Finnish Senate composed only of Russians was formed. And by 1910, all important Finnish legislation came from the Russian Duma (legislative assembly).

WORLD WAR I (1914-1918)

Finland was not a major player in World War I, but it did have some involvement, on both sides. At the beginning of the war, Russia deployed approximately 35, 0000 soldiers to Finland. This was a prophylactic move by Russia due to Finland's close proximity to Russia's capital of St. Petersburg (then still called Petrograd), and Russia's fear of a possible German invasion involving Finland's territory.

While many Finns demonstrated loyalty to the Russian Empire at the beginning of WWI, that soon was chipped away at by what the Finns viewed as oppressive measures and yet another Russian endeavor at their complete assimilation. The possibility of forming a volunteer unit for the German army crystalized amongst students at the University of Helsinki. After negotiations with German representatives and formal acceptance by German military authorities, in January 1915 these young Finnish activists began organizing a clandestine recruitment. The Russian authorities became aware of the movement and some of the young men were jailed in the Shpalernaya prison in Petrograd. It was then that this group became known as *kalterijääkärit*, translated "behind-bars Jägers" ("jäger" meaning "hunter" or "huntsman" in German) and the military unit became known as the Jäger Battalion.

In May 1915, approximately 2,000 Finnish volunteers crossed the border to Sweden, continuing on to Germany. A year later, the Jäger Battalion was fighting on the Eastern Front, much to the chagrin of the Russians. But the majority of Finland's political class still maintained loyalty to Russia, believing it to be beneficial to the Finnish.

INDEPENDENCE (1917)

In the midst of World War I, the Russian Revolution of 1917 occurred, marking one of the most explosive political events of the twentieth century. Led by Vladimir Lenin, the Bolsheviks (which would later become the Communist Party of the Soviet Union) seized power and ended centuries of Russian Imperial rule. The way was paved for the rise of communism, as well as the rise of the Soviet Union as a world power.

The Russian Revolution of 1917 actually consisted of two separate revolutions: the February and October Revolutions. Following the February Revolution, Russian Tsar Nicholas II abdicated, which Finland viewed as a dissolution of the legal union between Russia and Finland. Tsar Nicholas II had been the Grand Duke of Finland as well. Negotiations began between Finnish authorities and the new Russian Provisional Government, and by way of the so-called "Power Act," the Finnish Parliament declared itself to hold all legislative powers other than those regarding foreign policy and military issues. It also declared it could only be dissolved by its own action. Nevertheless, the Russian Provisional Government did dissolve the Finnish Parliament shortly thereafter.

During the October Revolution (of the 1917 Revolution), the Provisional Government was defeated. Immediately thereafter, the Finnish Parliament created a three-man regency council. The council was never elected, however, due to strong opposition by Finnish socialists. On November 15, 1917, the Bolsheviks declared the right of complete secession "for the Peoples of Russia." And on the same date, the Finnish Parliament issued a declaration pursuant to which it assumed, *pro tem*, all the powers of a sovereign Finland.

Under the leadership of Chairman Pehr Evind Svinhufvud, on November 27 the Finnish Senate began the work of executing independence as soon as possible. Political leaders had long felt that monarchism and heredity nobility were antiquated and advocated for a republican constitution. Therefore, when the Senate submitted to Parliament a Declaration of Independence on December 4, it was accompanied by a proposal for a new republican Instrument of Government.

Two days later, on December 6, 1917, Parliament adopted the Declaration. With reference to the November 15 declaration, the new declaration stated in part: "The people of Finland feel deeply that they cannot fulfil their national and international duty without complete sovereignty… The people of Finland dare to confidently await how other nations in the world recognize that with their full independence and freedom, the people of Finland can do their best in fulfilment of those purposes that will win them a place amongst civilized peoples."

Svinhufvud then immediately requested of Sweden, Germany, France, Denmark, and Norway a recognition of Finland's independence. They declined, however, until Finland's former ruler, Russia, did so. Svinhufvud was instructed to communicate with Lenin's Bolshevik Government, but Svinhufvud did not want to recognize the Bolsheviks as the legal ruler of Russia. Germany was in the midst of peace negotiations with Soviet Russia and encouraged the Finns to talk to Lenin and the Council of People's Commissars. Anxious for Germany's approval as soon as possible, Svinhufvud complied with this request.

On December 18, the Soviet Russian government formally recognized Finland's independence, and on December 22 it was approved by Lenin and the highest Soviet executive body, the All-Russian Central Executive Committee. On January 4, 1918, Germany, Sweden, and France followed suit; then Norway and Denmark on January 10; and Austria-Hungary on January 13.

* * *

On November 11, 1918, Germany and the Allies signed an armistice marking the end of World War I. When the Allies gathered to discuss the subsequent peace treaty that would be signed, Germany and Austria-Hungary were not invited. They were gratuitously allowed to present a response, one that was largely ignored. The subsequent Treaty of Versailles, executed June 28, 1919, contained a provision wherein Lithuania, Latvia, and Czechoslovakia, as well as Finland, were recognized as independent countries.

Although not directly related to Finland, several other provisions of the Treaty of Versailles worth mentioning are as follows:

- Poland also became an independent country with a "route to the sea" — a corridor of land that cut Germany in half.

- Austria-Hungary was split up and Yugoslavia was created.

- The German Army was cut to 100,000 troops, the German Navy to thirty-six ships and no submarines, and the German Air Force banned altogether.

- Pursuant to the "war guilt" clause, Germany had to accept complete blame for the war and also had to pay £6,600 million in reparations.

- To prevent further world conflict, a League of Nations was to be created.

Understandably, most Germans resented this "diktat" (dictated peace) and those who signed it were branded "the November Criminals." Britain and France wanted even harsher terms imposed on the Germans but overall felt the treaty was fair. And because the United States did not want to be part of the League of Nations, the country refused to ratify it. As a result, the League of Nations was fatally weakened without the U.S. and its military to enforce decisions.

FINNISH CIVIL WAR (01/27/1918 – 05/16/1918)

Any anticipated period of peace for newly independent Finland was short-lived. After the formal ties to Russia were cut, the internal struggle for power continued to intensify. Two factions had emerged: the Reds (or labor movement), who received support from Russia; and the Whites (or government troops), who received support from Germany. Triggered by the proclamation of independence, the Finnish Civil War immediately ensued.

Most research indicates that the true impetuses for the war were the lack of centralized political authority in the newly independent country, as well as the terrible plight of the poor in Finland. The dissatisfied tenant farmers working the landowners' properties in the countryside, along with overworked and underpaid factory workers in the cities, combined to create a perfect breeding ground for the seeds of socialist ideology. With the pull-out of the Russian administration following Finland's independence, the country lacked an army, police, and other similar institutions that perhaps could have quelled the rising tensions.

On January 27, 1918, the Reds seized power in Helsinki and declared a revolution. Led by General Gustaf Mannerheim, the conservative Whites initially fled to the western part of the country. At the outset of the war, around 40,000 Russian troops were still garrisoned on the western coast of Finland, and the Whites immediately set about disarming them.

The Red military employed approximately 100,000 men and women at its strongest, of which around 80% were in arms (including as many as 2,000 women). They occupied the industrialized southern part of Finland. The White troops, numbering 80,000-90,000 men, occupied mostly rural northern areas. In February, approximately 1,200 Finnish Jägers returned to Finland to join the fight with the Whites. They had been in Germany since 1915 when they became involved in World War I, and had been being trained by the German Army ever since. Their combat experience and leadership were of tremendous aid to the Whites.

The Reds, having secured control of the south, held the military lead until mid-March, but the Whites were gaining momentum. In early April, the Whites sought to establish German positions around the Gulf of Finland. In support of this endeavor, 10,000 men from the German Baltic Sea Division, as well as the detachment Brandenstein of 3,000 men, landed in southern Finland.

Although the Finnish Civil War certainly began as an internal struggle, once the Germans intervened, southern Finland became a theater of World War I. On April 13, the Germans re-took Helsinki, and the final decisive battle ended with the Whites' conquest of Vyborg on April 29. On May 16, the White victory was formally declared.

Even though this conflict was short-lived, it resulted in a relatively large number of casualties. The death toll from the Finnish Civil War was far from concluded at the war's end, though, and actually doubled shortly thereafter. Swift trials of former revolutionaries were had, followed by harsh sentences. Approximately 20,000 Reds were either executed or died in prison camps from hunger and the Spanish flu epidemic, increasing the total war-related deaths to almost 40,000. A few of the revolutionary leaders who were able to escape to Soviet Russia later founded the Finnish Communist Party in Moscow. Yet others continued on, fleeing to western Europe and/or the United States.

The Kinship Wars (1918-1922)

Also known as "the Heimosodat," the Finnish Kinship Wars are relatively unknown outside of Finland because there is almost nothing available about it in English. Almost 10,000 Finnish volunteers took part in these wars between 1918 and 1922. The objective was to bring under Finnish control the large areas between the White Sea and Finland that had predominantly Finn populations—to expand into what nationalists referred to as a "Greater Finland."

Remember that there had been a century of nationalist agitation culminating in Finland's Declaration of Independence in 1917. Many Finnish politicians viewed the area of Eastern Karelia in particular as one that should be a Finnish territory. On February 23, 1918, General Mannerheim issued his famous proclamation, "The Order of the Day of the Sword Scabbard," which said: *I will not put my sword in my scabbard before all the fortresses are in our hands, before constitutional order prevails in the country, not until the last warrior of Lenin and the last thug is deported and Finland includes White Sea Karelia.*

The Viena Expedition (1918)

The first attempt by Finnish volunteer forces to annex White Sea Karelia occurred in what was called the Viena Expedition. It was in the spring of 1918, and the Finnish Civil War was still ongoing.

The ultimate goal was to liberate White Karelia and establish the border.

Upon the Finnish troops' arrival in White Sea Karelia, they discovered a population divided between: one, those who wanted to secede from Russia and form an independent Karelia; two, a larger part that just wanted autonomy; and three, only a small minority that wanted Karelia to be a part of Finland. But what was of utmost importance for the vast majority of the population were practical issues, such has having enough food.

By June 1918, the British/American Murmansk Expeditionary Force was growing in Eastern Karelia, as they were starting recruitment campaigns among the Finnish Red Guards who were continuing their civil war against the Finnish volunteers. The Finns' Viena expedition began to deteriorate. There was no question that the Brits' military force was the strongest in the region, and the Finnish volunteers learned that their efforts to provoke a revolt in the locals against the Russians were not working. Further, the British were able to provide bread and rifles to anyone willing to enlist with them, while the Finns had little to offer except their nationalist ideologies. By the fall of 1918, the Viena Expedition forces were forced to retreat.

The Aunus Expedition (1919-1920)

After the failed Viena Expedition, a number of refugees fled to Finland from Eastern Karelia that winter, reporting that the Bolsheviks were forcefully taking men and food in the town of Aunus for the benefit of the Red Army. Also, the end of the Finnish Civil War had freed up troops, equipment, and weapons. In February 1919, General Mannerheim (who had been named as the Regent of Finland as well) planned an attack of the Bolsheviks in St. Petersburg. His plan included material and moral support from Britain, the Karelians, and the White Russians.

The Aunus Expedition was fraught with issues from the start. One, as a result of the various factions represented, there was a constant power struggle as well as an unclear chain of command for the troops. Two, only a few local Karelians joined the Finnish troops. Three, although the British were allied with the Russian Whites against the Bolsheviks, this did not necessarily translate into them supporting a "Greater Finland." Four, even though the Finnish government "supported" the expedition, no military troops were provided to the volunteer force, and ultimately the State would not even send needed supplies for fear of Soviet reaction. The all-volunteer Aunus Expedition was severely under-manned and unequipped, resulting in failure.

The Treaty of Tartu (October 1920)

After four months of negotiations, a peace treaty between Russia and Finland was signed on October 14, 1920. During negotiations, Finland proposed that the residents of the coveted Eastern Karelia be able to choose, through a referendum, whether they would be a Finnish or Soviet territory. The Soviets refused.

Pursuant to the Tartu Treaty, Finland renounced its territorial claims to Karelia, but Karelia was to be able to at least maintain cultural autonomy. The Finns did gain the port of Petsamo. The treaty also formally annulled the Russian-Swedish Treaty of Fredrikshamn (1809) under which Finland had been included in the Russian Empire. Interestingly, each party received the text of the Tartu Treaty in four languages: Russian, Finnish, Swedish, and French.

The East Karelian Uprising (1921-1922)

After only a few months under the Bolshevik regime, there was tremendous unrest and dissatisfaction with the Soviets. In mid-October 1921, a group of Eastern Karelian rebels met and voted in favor of secession from Soviet Russia. This time, the initiative was taken by the Karelians, but Finnish volunteers joined in (though mostly in leadership positions). The Karelians had expected Finland's military to intervene, which did not occur; but the Finnish government did supply humanitarian aid.

In November, the Karelian invasion began. By the end of December, they had made significant advancement, but the Soviets had gotten wind of the Finnish government's "support" in the form of volunteers and aid. The Red Army's Commander, Leon Trotsky, announced that he would march towards Helsinki. Around the same time, approximately 20,000 Red Army troops—including Red Finns who fled to Soviet Russia after their defeat in the Finnish Civil War—mounted a counterattack in Karelia. The grossly outnumbered

Karelian rebels were crushed by January 1922. The last unit of the uprising fled on February 16. By the end of the uprising, approximately 30,000 East Karelian refugees had evacuated to Finland.

The two countries (Finland and Soviet Russia) signed yet another agreement in Helsinki on June 1, 1922, providing for the inviolability of the Soviet-Finnish border. A famous Bolshevik propaganda poster from 1922 read: "We don't want war, but we will defend the Soviets!"

Interwar Period (1919-1939)

Finland – A Republic (1919)

Almost immediately following the conclusion of the Civil War, it was decided to make Finland a monarchy. In October 1918, a German prince (not surprisingly) was chosen as king: Frederick Charles of Hessen. Shortly thereafter, though, with Germany's defeat in WWI, General Mannerheim was designated as regent, and was also assigned the task of creating a proposal for a new constitution. It was obvious that Finland would be a republic but the question and struggle surrounded presidential power.

The Conservatives wanted the president's powers to be independent of Parliament, but the reorganized Social Democrats and other liberal parties wanted most powers placed in Parliament. As a result of the Conservatives' strong post-Civil War position, they were successful in pushing through a relatively authoritative president chosen by popularly-elected representatives and independent of Parliament.

Finland's new constitution was confirmed on July 17, 1919. Despite the Conservatives' prior victory, the Social Democrats, aligned with the National Progressive Party, were able to defeat the Conservative candidate Mannerheim. The National Progressive Party leader, Kaarlo Juho Ståhlberg, was elected as the first president of Finland on July 25, 1919.

* * *

The 1919 Constitution established Finnish as a national language, along with Swedish. But for the younger generation who wanted Finnish to be supreme, this was not sufficient. As more Finnish speakers gained positions of power, the strength of the Swedish language weakened. This language controversy continued until after World War II, when the relevant laws were revised. The current constitution provides equal status for the Finnish language as Swedish, and also, Swedish is a required subject in Finnish schools.

During the years between wars (prior to the start of WWII in 1939), Finland was very much an agrarian country, certainly more so than the rest of the Nordic countries. As much as 70% of the population worked in the arenas of agriculture and forestry. Consequently, paper and items manufactured from wood were Finland's primary export commodities. The Smallholdings Law of 1918 and further land reform in 1922 attempted to give tenant farmers and landless laborers their own small parcels of land; as a result, almost 100,000 "smallholdings" were created. Those independent smallholders formed the majority of the Agrarian Party (now the Centre Party), which from that period forward has been a major player in Finnish politics.

Following Ståhlberg's presidency (1919-25), the Agrarian Party's candidate, Lauri Kristian Relander, was elected. The Social Democratic Party, however, maintained the majority representation in the Parliament throughout the first decade of Finnish independence. The leftist wing of the Social Democrats separated from the party in the early 1920s, advocating communism, and successfully won twenty-seven Parliamentary seats in the 1922 election. All of these representatives ultimately were arrested for treason on the grounds of "revolutionary intent."

LAPUA MOVEMENT (1929-1932)

In 1929, something known as the Lapua Movement began in Finland. It was dominated by radical anti-communist nationalists, and named after the town of Lapua in which it was founded. Anti-communism sentiment was definitely prevalent in the educated classes after the Finnish Civil War; however, the Lapua Movement advocated the use of violence to suppress communism, resulting in a decrease in its popularity over time.

In November 1929, meetings and protests of the Young Communist League of Finland in Lapua provoked the Finnish nationalists, resulting in the first anti-communist meeting of the Lapua Movement with more than a thousand people in attendance. They took the position that the communists had "mocked God, the Lutheran Church, the 'bourgeois' fatherland, the Finnish army, and General Mannerheim." A violent response to the Young Communist League's agitation ensued.

As the movement's numbers grew, meetings and protests were arranged throughout the country. In June 1930, communist printing presses were destroyed in Oulu and Vaasa. On July 7, more than 12,000 men marched on Helsinki in what was a major show of power for the movement; it was referred to as the "Peasant March."

The Finnish government reacted to Lapua pressure by outlawing communist newspapers in a "Protection of the Republic Act."

The Lapua Movement became increasingly violent. They often administered a treatment called "muilutus," where the subject was kidnapped, beaten, thrown into a car, driven to the border of the Soviet Union, and dropped off. But tragically for many of these Finns who remained in the Soviet Union, they were later accused by Stalin of being "Nationalists" and executed during the Great Purge.

In February 1932, armed Lapua activists violently interrupted a Social Democrat meeting in Mäntsälä. This incident escalated to an attempted coup d'état, which became known as the Mäntsälä Rebellion. General Wallenius, the former Chief of Staff of Finland's army, led the rebellion but was largely unable to obtain support from the Finnish army and the Whites. President Svinhufvud subsequently gave a radio speech to those in the movement which essentially put an end to the rebellion. On November 21, 1932, the Lapua Movement was banned, ironically under the Protection of the Republic Act, which the movement had worked to get passed.

Finnish Neutrality

The Finnish government and country as a whole clearly took the position that a neutral foreign policy doctrine was best during the interwar period. They were said to seek "friendship toward all and alliances with none." During the 1930s, the Finns' relations with the United States continued to grow stronger. Finland endorsed several

U.S. proposals regarding international peace and international commercial measures.

The Finnish understandably remained fearful of Soviet designs, and the Soviets were concerned that their neighboring Finland could be used as a springboard for an invasion. During the Japanese invasion of Manchuria in September 1931 (considered to be the first step towards the start of World War II), the Soviet Union started negotiations for a non-aggression pact with its neighboring countries of Finland, Estonia, Latvia, and Poland; Finland signed it on January 21, 1932.

World War II Era (1939-1945)

On August 23, 1939, Germany and the Soviet Union signed the Molotov-Ribbentrop Pact, officially known as the "Treaty of Non-Aggression between Germany and the Union of Soviet Socialist Republics." In the portion that was publicized, it stated that the agreement was reached to "strengthen[ ] the cause of peace between Germany and the U.S.S.R." Both parties agreed to "desist from any act of violence, any aggressive action, and any attack on each other," among other things.

As part of a "Secret Additional Protocol," however, the borders of Soviet and German spheres of influence across Finland, Poland, Lithuania, Latvia, and Estonia were defined. Specifically, it provided:

- In the event of a rearrangement—territorial and political—of the areas of the Baltic States, the northern boundary of Lithuania would represent the boundary between the "spheres of influence" of the U.S.S.R. and Germany.
- In the event of a similar rearrangement of the areas belonging to the Polish state, the line of the Rivers Narev, Vistula, and San would represent the boundary between the "spheres of influence" of the two countries.
- A determination as to whether the maintenance of an independent Polish state would be desirable and how it

would be bounded was to be made during further discussions between the governments, but would be ultimately resolved with a "friendly agreement."

- Both parties were to treat the protocol as "strictly secret."

Therefore, pursuant to the above, Finland was deemed to belong to the Soviet sphere of interest. The existence of "The Secret Protocol" was just a rumor until it became public during the famous post-WWII Nuremberg trials.

Within a week of the aforementioned Molotov-Ribbentrop Pact being finalized, Germany invaded Poland (September 1, 1939); this is considered by many to be the date of the start of World War II. The way this invasion was orchestrated was a foreshadowing of the Soviet invasion of Finland just two months later, commencing the Winter War.

To justify Germany's invasion of Poland, Hitler falsely claimed that the Poles were persecuting ethnic Germans. In collusion with the German military, on August 31, 1939, at approximately 8:00 p.m., Nazi SS troops donned Polish uniforms and staged a phony Polish attack on a German radio station. Just over eight hours later, at 4:45 a.m. on September 1, a million and a half million Germans invaded Poland, launching a "retaliatory" campaign against them.

Approximately two weeks later, on September 17, Stalin ordered the Soviet invasion of Poland. The new border between the German and Soviet powers had already been established by the aforementioned "Secret Additional Protocol" of the Molotov-Ribbentrop Pact (that part which became known as "the German-Soviet Frontier Treaty").

Russo-Finnish / Winter War (1939-1940)

In October 1939, Stalin gained control of the Baltic states, i.e., Latvia, Lithuania, and Estonia. Confident that he could then obtain control of Finland without much effort, Stalin then demanded the islands of the Gulf of Finland, territories on the Karelian Isthmus, and a military base near Helsinki. The Finns refused, again (as similar demands had been made in prior years as well).

While many people are familiar with the aforementioned details of Germany's invasion of Poland, most people are unaware that Finland's invasion by the Soviets was taken from the same playbook. On November 26, 1939, the Soviets accused the Finnish army of shelling the Soviet border post of Mainila. In reality, it was Soviet NKVD agents (the forerunner of the KGB) who staged the attack in an attempt to justify reneging on nonaggression treaties with Finland. Just four days later, the Red Army attacked Finland.

Commencing what became known as the Winter War (or Russo-Finnish War), on November 30, 1939, Stalin invaded Finland, marching across the Finnish-Soviet border as well as conducting a simultaneous aerial bombing of Helsinki. But the Soviet Foreign Minister, Vyacheslav Molotov, at first claimed that any reports of a Soviet bombing were not true, but that what had actually been dropped were groceries and other humanitarian supplies. A precursor to the "Molotov cocktail," the Finns dubbed the Soviet bombs "Molotov's bread baskets."

The clear intent of the Soviets was an ultimate annexation of Finland into the U.S.S.R., which would include the liberation of the "Red Finns." One would think that the "Goliath" of the Soviet superpower would have quickly and handily defeated the Finnish "David." With troops of almost 400,000—almost three times greater than the number of Allied landing at Normandy—the Red Army marched across the border with what should have been an instant and decisive victory.

During the first few days, a thousand Soviet tanks successfully occupied large tracts of Finland's forests as the Finns did not have the necessary anti-tank ammunition to adequately combat them. But Finnish engineers discovered a vulnerable exhaust opening on the Red Army's T-28 tanks. Wearing white uniforms to blend into the snow, Finnish ski troopers silently wove through the trees and tossed improvised incendiary grenades through the openings and into the tanks, causing them to explode from the inside out.

The grenades were made from a vodka bottle that contained a flammable liquid mix (gasoline, kerosene, or any combination of explosive liquid chemicals), topped with a flammable rag in the opening. Because the Finns had decided that Molotov and all of his Red Army friends needed a drink to go along with their "Molotov bread baskets," the "Molotov cocktail" was born.

Stalin's army was forced to switch strategies. On December 6, 1939, they mounted a large-scale infantry invasion with a huge number advantage. This time, as each wave of Soviet soldiers advanced in the snow, the Finnish ski troopers mowed them down with expertly-positioned automatic weapons. The quantity of dead Soviet soldiers, combined with sub-zero temperatures which hardened the corpses, allowed the Red Army to utilize their own piled-up dead for cover from Finnish machine gun rounds.

Less than a month into the conflict, seven entire Soviet infantry divisions and 250 T-28 tanks had been wiped out. And in the meantime, a bitter winter had brought temperatures as low as negative forty degrees Fahrenheit. Both sides were forced to withdraw and regroup in January 1940 during the unbearable cold.

Having learned from their monumental mistakes, the Red Army returned in February with an all-out assault: forty-five divisions for a total of 750,000 troops. By mid-March, the Finnish troops were almost out of ammunition, and an agreement between the two countries was reached, memorialized in what was known as the Moscow Peace Treaty. It is estimated that the Red Army lost more than 200,000 soldiers, with the Finns losing less than 50,000 of their own. To put an end to the fighting, however, Finland sacrificed some of its border territories in a "defeat" wherein they maintained their independence, as well as gained global admiration.

Relevant portions of the Moscow Peace Treaty were as follows:

- Hostilities between the two countries were to cease immediately.
- The boundary between Finland and the U.S.S.R. was to run along a new line in such a way that the entire Karelian Isthmus would be included in the territory of the U.S.S.R.
- Both countries would refrain from attacking the other, as well as from making any alliance directed against either of the countries.
- For a period of thirty years, Finland agreed to lease to the Soviet Union the area of Hanko Cape and the surrounding waters for an annual rental rate of eight million Finnish marks; the Soviet Union was to utilize said territory for the establishment of a naval base that also would serve to defend the mouth of the Gulf of Finland against attack.
- The U.S.S.R. would withdraw their troops from the Petsamo area, the same that they had already ceded to Finland pursuant to the peace treaty of 1920. But the Soviets were given the right of free transit across this area to Norway and back, and they could establish a consulate in the area as well.
- Also pursuant to the same 1920 peace treaty, Finland was to refrain from maintaining warships and other armed ships in the waters along the coast of the Arctic Ocean.
- Finland granted to the Soviets the right to transport goods (across / through Finland) between the

Soviet Union and Sweden. Both countries acknowledged the necessity of building upon their own territory(ies) a railway that would connect Kantalahti (Kandalaksha) with Kemijärvi, with as much as possible to be completed in the year 1940.

- Economic relations between the countries were to be restored, including entering into negotiations for a formal trade agreement.

The Moscow Peace Treaty between Finland and the U.S.S.R. was signed on March 12, 1940. But the "peace" did not last long.

THE CONTINUATION WAR (1941-1944)

In the months that followed, despite the perceived protection of the peace treaty, Soviets continued to meddle in Finnish affairs. For example, although not required by the treaty, the Soviets demanded the demilitarization of the Finnish Aland Islands, as well as demanded to send their troop trains through Finnish territory. In June and July of 1940, the Soviets annexed the Baltic States, and the Finns feared they would be next. It appears this fear was not without basis; it was reported that the Soviet Foreign Minister Molotov had privately admitted to German hosts during a late-1940 trip to Berlin that the Soviets intended to "crush" Finland.

Unbeknownst to the Soviets, Finland had entered into an agreement with Germany (first in August 1940, followed by a further agreement in December of the same year). Pursuant to the same,

Finland obtained material and military assistance from Germany, and Hitler obtained a staging base in Finland for his subsequent invasion of the Soviet Union. Most historians agree that Finland's motivation for this involvement with Nazi Germany was different than most other countries joining SS foreign volunteers. One author stated: "At the beginning of the attack (on the Soviet Union), Finns were unaware of the Germans' goal of eradicating the Jews. Finns were, above all, interested in fighting against the Soviet Union." Or, another author opined: "The consequences of being conquered by Stalin were much worse (for Finns) than being an ally of Hitler, so they chose the lesser evil."

The Finnish military joined the Nazis in planning for an invasion of Russia in 1941. However, it was not considered to be "politically expedient" for Finland to participate in the June 22 German invasion. Three days later, after Soviet aerial attacks of Finland, the Finnish government had a legitimate basis for open hostilities, i.e., defending itself against an act of Soviet aggression. Thus, war was declared on June 26, aptly called "The Continuation War" by the Finns, as it was seen as a continuation of the Winter War.

The Finnish Army immediately began a major offensive and by the end of August 1941 their troops had reached the pre-war boundaries. By the end of the year, the front had become stabilized, and no further major offensive operations were conducted for two-and-a-half years.

Despite Finland's co-belligerence with Axis Germany, the Western Allies recognized that Finland was fighting its own separate war against the Soviet Union. As stated above, it is undisputed that the Finnish government never appeared to have any intent of participating in the systematic killing of Jews. Not only were Jews tolerated in Finland, but Jewish refugees were even allowed asylum, garnering the Finns tremendous respect in the West. And Finland did not conduct military operations against any Allied country other than the Soviet Union.

After the aforementioned period of more than two years of no Finnish military offensives, and after the disastrous German defeat at Stalingrad in February 1943, Finland began to seek an exit from the war. There were intermittent negotiations in 1943 and 1944 between, on the one side, the Western Allies and the Soviet Union, and Finland on the other. When no agreement was reached, in June 1944 the Soviets launched a powerful offensive against Finnish positions that appeared to threaten the country's independence and survival. Wisely, Finnish leaders decided to pledge future friendship—or at least neutrality—with the Soviet Union, and essentially "apologized." Fortuitously for Finland, Stalin turned his attention to Poland and the Balkans.

Despite Finland's stabilization of their front once again, an exhausted country even more desperately wanted out of the war. On September 19, 1944, a peace agreement known as the Moscow Armistice was signed between the Soviet Union and U.K. on one side, and Finland on the other. Essentially, it restored the aforementioned Moscow Peace Treaty of 1940, but with a number of modifications. Among other things, it provided for:

- the Finns ceding to the Soviets: all of Petsamo, parts of Karelia and Salla, and certain islands in the Gulf of Finland;

- the expulsion of all German troops from Finnish territory;

- a restriction in the size of the Finnish armed forces;

- the Finns' leasing of the Porkkala Peninsula to the Soviets for a period of fifty years;

- the Finns' abolition of various "rightist" or fascist organizations and recognition of the legal status of The Communist Party of Finland;

- the Finns' payment of war reparations to the Soviet Union (the equivalent of $300 million USD in the form of various commodities, approximately $4.5 billion USD in today's dollars).

No doubt, Finland did not view its second "defeat" by the Red Army as a total loss. The country still maintained its coveted independence as a democratic nation directly on the border of the Soviet Union.

As a quite interesting and impressive side note, out of all the countries that were required to pay reparations from World War II, as of 2015, Finland was the only one known to have paid its bill in full, which it did in 1952.

THE LAPLAND WAR (1944-1945)

Ironically, the ending of the Continuation War sparked another, albeit much less destructive, war for Finland: the Lapland War. Nazi Germany refused to leave Finland, their main interest being the Petsamo nickel mines in the northernmost Lapland region that had been ceded by Finland to the Soviets. In 1934, it was estimated that these mines contained more than five million tons of nickel, and nickel was of great importance in the production of arms and munitions.

The fighting between the Germans and Finns was initially somewhat hesitant, most likely due to their previous alliance against the Soviets. They fairly quickly reached an informal agreement wherein the German troops were scheduled to evacuate from Lapland to Norway. The Soviets did not approve of Finland's niceties to and patience with the Nazis, though, and pressured the Finns to be more aggressive in pushing them out. When hostilities intensified, the Germans did retreat, but in a scorched-earth manner. Substantial areas of northern Finland were devastated and although the total death toll was relatively small—approximately 3,000 troops—around 100,000 Finns lost their homes. This obviously added to Finland's already heavy post-war reconstruction burden. In April

1945, the last of the German troops left Finnish soil, shortly before World War II came to a close.

END OF WWII (1945)

With the unconditional surrender of Germany in May 1945, World War II came to an end in Europe. On May 8, the Germans surrendered to the Western Allies (including the U.S. and Britain). But with the tenuous alliance between the U.S. and the Soviets already having turned "cold," the Soviets demanded their own surrender ceremony; therefore, on May 9, a separate surrender took place in Russia.

Subsequent Allied peace conferences split up the defeated German nation into four "Allied occupation zones." The eastern part of the country went to the Soviet Union, and the western to the United States, Great Britain, and (eventually) France. The city of Berlin was located entirely within the eastern Soviet part of the country, but the relevant agreements (Yalta and Potsdam) similarly split the city, i.e., the eastern half to the Soviets and the western to the other Allies—thus the four occupation zones.

In the East, the Japanese surrender occurred after the dropping of U.S. bombs on Hiroshima and Nagasaki on August 6 and 9, respectively. Japan surrendered unconditionally on August 14, 1945, and formalized it with their signature on September 2.

THE COLD WAR ERA (1945-1991)

Even though the United States and Russia were WWII allies against the Axis powers, as mentioned above, the relationship between the two nations had become quite tense. With the post-war Soviet expansion in Eastern Europe, both the Americans and British feared communism spreading into Western European democracies, as well as a permanent Soviet domination of Eastern Europe. On the other hand, the Soviets indeed were intent on spreading communism worldwide, as well as maintaining control of Eastern Europe. The state of political hostility between the U.S.-led Western powers and the Soviet bloc countries became known as the Cold War.

As set out previously herein, part of the Moscow Armistice ending the Continuation War in September 1944 required Finland to pay the Soviet Union substantial war reparations in the form of goods. These goods included not only raw materials but trains and ships as well. Consequently, Finland's metal and shipbuilding industries rapidly expanded, and Finland began to evolve from a mostly agrarian country into one that was more industrialized. Further, after Finland's debt was paid in full, the country benefited from continued trade with the Soviets, their timber exporting even exceeding pre-war levels.

Treaty of Friendship, Cooperation, and Mutual Assistance (1948)

Relations between Finland and the Soviet Union continued to stabilize with the maintenance of friendly policies on the part of Finnish presidents. In 1948, an appropriately named "Treaty of Friendship, Cooperation, and Mutual Assistance" (a.k.a. "YYA Treaty") was memorialized between the countries as an expression of their new foreign policy. The relevant provisions are set out below:

- In the event that Finland (or the Soviet Union through Finnish territory) were to be attacked by Germany or any of its allies, Finland would "fight to repel the attack," including using all its available forces by land, sea, and air.

- If necessary, the Soviet Union would assist or join Finland in their defense of Germany or its allies. (But strangely, the treaty provided that the giving of assistance by the Soviet Union would be "subject to mutual agreement" between the countries.)

- The parties reaffirmed their pledge not to participate in any alliance or coalition directed against the other.

- The parties expressed their assurance of cooperating towards the further development of economic and cultural relations between the two countries.

- The parties pledged to observe mutual respect of the other's sovereignty, as well as non-interference in the other's internal affairs.

NORTH ATLANTIC TREATY ORGANIZATION (NATO) (1949)

In an effort to guard against further communist expansion, the United States and eleven Western Europe nations formed the North Atlantic Treaty Organization (NATO) on April 4, 1949. The North Atlantic Treaty was signed on that date in Washington, D.C. by the foreign ministers of the following member countries: Belgium, Canada, Denmark, France, Iceland, Italy, Luxembourg, the Netherlands, Norway, Portugal, and the United Kingdom (as well as the U.S.).

At the heart of the North Atlantic Treaty is the principle of a common and collective defense, which is set out in the most well-known Article 5 of the same. It provides that any armed attack against any one of the parties (participating countries) "shall be considered an attack against them all." And if such an attack were to occur, each party will assist as necessary, "including the use of armed force, to restore the security of the North Atlantic area."

By 1952, Greece and Turkey had joined NATO, followed by the Federal Republic of Germany (West Germany) in 1955.

HELSINKI SUMMER OLYMPICS (1952)

1952 was quite significant in Finnish history. In addition to Finnish Armi Kuusela being crowned Miss Universe and Finland paying its last war reparations to the Soviets, Helsinki hosted the Summer Olympics. The Olympics were originally scheduled for 1940 in Japan, but in 1937 Japan forfeited, and due to the war, the games were delayed twelve years. The post-war proximity of only seven years was still evident in some ways. For example, sugar and coffee were still being rationed.

To date, Helsinki is the smallest city to have ever hosted the Summer Olympics. The 1952 games were officially known as "the Games of the XV Olympiad," and approximately 70,000 tourists converged upon Finland. What they discovered was a capital city that, even if post-war poor, was hospitable and modern. The buildings that had been constructed for the games were, and still are, internationally renowned for their minimalist architecture with concrete construction and simple and unadorned surfaces finished in white.

At the opening ceremony on July 19, 1952, 2,500 pigeons symbolizing peace were appropriately set free. And a Soviet Union team, which was entering Olympic competition for the very first time, won an amazing twenty-two gold medals. A prevalent theme in Helsinki has been "triumph over adversity."

THE WARSAW PACT (1955)

The Soviet Union and its affiliated communist nations in Eastern Europe formed a rival alliance to NATO: the Warsaw Pact. Although the Warsaw Pact certainly was in some ways a response to the creation of NATO, it really was more directly motivated by the Soviets' fear of Germany once again becoming a military power. The U.S. and other NATO countries had advocated making West Germany part of their alliance, and also allowing it to form an army.

The re-militarization of West Germany, and it formally joining NATO on May 5, 1955, prompted the signing of the Warsaw Pact less than two weeks later on May 14. The countries joining the U.S.S.R. in the Warsaw Pact were: Albania, Czechoslovakia, the German Democratic Republic (East Germany), Hungary, Poland, and Romania. Nearly every European nation was now solidly aligned in one or the other of these opposing camps, formalizing the post-WWII, "Cold War" political division of the European continent. Finland was not one of them.

"FINDLANDIZATION"

During the Cold War, Finland officially followed a policy of neutrality. West German scholars coined the somewhat derisive term "Findlandization" to describe the country's efforts to maintain good relations with their Soviet (and giant) neighbor. A prime example was Finland's refusal to join NATO. But Finland also tried to keep good relations with the West with their officially neutral Cold War position. The term "Findlandization" became commonly used, and still is, in reference to a small country that allows a larger and more powerful neighboring country to significantly influence its policies.

Despite criticism from some, Finland's cautious and realistic foreign policy ultimately earned the country recognition. In 1955 Finland joined two very important organizations: the United Nations (UN) and the Nordic Council. Their international profile began to be one of a country that cultivated peace and stability. The United States' policy in regard to Finland was to support the country in remaining an independent, sovereign, and democratic state, and of course the U.S. supported its membership in the United Nations.

After the Soviet invasion of Hungary in 1956, Finland's balancing act with Russia became even more delicate. The Soviets had brutally attacked the Hungarians—killing approximately 30,000 people in only ten days—after which Soviet rule was restored. Finland desperately sought to engage with Moscow without offending Western allies. As one University of Helsinki political science professor put it, "The whole political life went overboard in terms of friendliness to the Soviets."

There can be no doubt that there were Finns who crossed the line of "friendliness" with the Soviets into true espionage. One young Finnish journalist, Matts Dumell, was charged with such, and ultimately served an eight-month prison sentence for treason as a result. There is rumored to be a secret list of eighteen others locked in a safe of the Finland Security Police (SUPO); it is called the "Tiitenen list," named after Seppo Tiitenen, a former director of the

SUPO. This notorious list is of tremendous interest to those debating how Finland's elite cultivated friendships with communist regimes in order to maintain peace with the Soviets.

Despite the YYA Treaty giving the Soviet Union some authority in Finnish domestic policies, Finland was able to maintain capitalism, unlike most other Soviet-bordering countries. After a period of failed experimentation with protectionism in the 1950s, it began to ease trade restrictions. In 1961, Finland became a member of the European Free Trade Association (EFTA). The year prior, the EFTA had been established as an alternative trade bloc for European states that were unable or unwilling to join the then European Economic Community (EEC, which subsequently became the European Union). In 1973, Finland joined the EEC.

The Berlin Wall (1961-1989)

The post-WWII existence of the capitalist city of West Berlin deep within communist East Germany "stuck like a bone in the Soviet throat," as it was put by Soviet leader Nikita Khrushchev. Post-war tension between the Russians on the one side and the U.S., Britain, and France on the other escalated as the Russians maneuvered to drive their former allies out of the Berlin. Over the next decade—while negotiations at various summits and conferences took place without resolution—literally millions of East Germans fled from east to west.

On the evening of August 12, 1961, after the largest number of defectors crossed from East to West Berlin in a single day, Russian

Premier Kruschev gave East Germany permission to close the border for good, and within two weeks, a makeshift barbed-wire and concrete-block wall—the infamous Berlin Wall.

Between 1961 and 1989, it was impossible to get from East to West Berlin except through armed checkpoints along the wall, and it was rarely allowed other than under extraordinary circumstances. Of course, this did not altogether prevent escape from East Germany. During this approximate twenty-eight-year period, more than 5,000 East Germans successfully crossed the border. But, at least 171 people were killed trying.

The Berlin Wall is quite relevant to Finland's history as it not only divided the city of Berlin, and the country of Germany, but also in many ways, all of Europe and even the world.

The Helsinki Accords (1975)

Finland had come to enjoy its global respect and status as a western democratic country that was friendly with the Soviet Union. As such, it began to push for a reduction of the military and political tensions of the Cold War. The Conference on Security and Co-operation in Europe was formed to serve as a forum for dialogue and negotiation between the West and the East, and beginning in 1973, met for a period of over two years in Helsinki. The Helsinki Final Act (a.k.a. the "Helsinki Accords") was signed on August 1, 1975, intended to improve relations between the communists and the West. Thirty-five countries signed it, including the United States, Canada, and all European countries except Albania and Andorra.

The Helsinki Accords had what were called three major "baskets." First, both sides agreed to recognize the then-current borders of European countries. Second, both sides agreed to respect human rights and freedoms in their respective countries. Third, both sides agreed to help each other in the areas of economics and technology. Further, in the "Decalogue" (or "Declaration on Principles Guiding Relations Between Participating States"), the Helsinki Final Act set out ten fundamental principles intended to govern the behavior of states towards their citizens, as well as towards each other:

1. Sovereign equality, respect for the rights inherent in sovereignty;
2. Refraining from the threat or use of force;
3. Inviolability of frontiers;
4. Territorial integrity of States;
5. Peaceful settlement of disputes;
6. Non-intervention in internal affairs;
7. Respect for human rights and fundamental freedoms, including the freedom of thought, conscience, religion or belief;
8. Equal rights and self-determination of peoples;
9. Co-operation among States;
10. Fulfilment in good faith of obligations under international law.

Collapse of the Soviet Union (1991)

On November 9, 1989, as the Cold War had finally begun to thaw across Eastern Europe, East Berlin's Communist Party's spokesman announced that at midnight, their citizens were free to cross the borders. Over the following weekend, more than two million people from East Berlin visited West Berlin for what one journalist called "the greatest street party in the history of the world." People also began using hammers and picks to begin tearing down the wall, and with the aid of cranes and bulldozers, it was soon gone.

This almost-thirty-year-old barrier between East and West Germany had symbolized the Cold War division of Europe. Aptly, one Berliner spray-painted on a piece of the wall: *Only today is the war really over.* On October 3, 1990, almost one year after the fall of the physical wall, East and West Germany were officially reunified, and the swift collapse of the other East European regimes was triggered. On December 25, 1991, with the resignation of the Soviet General Secretary of the Communist Party, Mikhail Gorbachev, the Union of Soviet Socialist Republics of dissolved.

Finland's Great Depression (1990-1994)

Since Finland had conducted so much trade with the Soviets for decades, the collapse of the Soviet Union was devastating to the Finnish economy. But this was not the only blame for the depression;

a banking crisis was as well. Throughout the 1980s, Finland had enjoyed a strong economic boom, resulting in Finns using foreign credit to invest in real estate markets and stocks. Soaring prices enticed banks, individual investors, private companies, and even workers' unions to participate in speculative activities, believing that they would get rich exploiting these bubbles. The economic crisis that ensued in Finland has been considered to be one of the worst in an industrialized country since World War II.

When the economy crashed, the unemployment rate climbed from 3% to 18% within four years. The GDP fell by 13%. Tens of thousands of households had serious debt problems, and there was a wave of bankruptcies. In order to save the country's economy, the Bank of Finland was forced to allow the markka to "float," abandoning the policy of a fixed exchange rate. The government also took over the savings bank group that had suffered the biggest losses, and ultimately downsized and restructured the banking industry.

In the midst of the depression, the government boldly decided to invest heavily in innovation ecosystems that paid off very quickly; in information technologies, Finland was to become a world leader. And with the painful measures taken by the Finns, the foundation had been laid for a strong economy from the latter half of the decade onwards.

Modern-Day Finland

European Union (EU)

In 1994, a referendum in Finland confirmed that the majority of the population (almost 57%) was in favor of joining the EU. They no doubt realized that membership would strengthen their international position and the security of the country, and it really was a very logical step in Finland's post-WWII western integration.

On January 1, 1995, Finland officially became a member of the EU, along with Austria and Sweden on the same date. With this action, Finland generally abandoned its prior long-standing policy of neutrality, as it was now part of this "political union." As a result, Finland gained more export access to the wider EU market. And of course, yet another benefit from Finland joining the EU when it did was an added layer of protection against its post-communist and rather unstable neighbor of Russia.

Finland is also a party to the Schengen Agreement, a treaty that prompted most of the European countries to abolish their borders. Many Finnish people, particularly the younger generations, saw the personal and professional benefits that free mobility across EU borders would provide.

In Finn President Martti Ahtisaari's 1999 New Year's speech, he expressed that primarily thanks to his country's membership in the EU, Finland's international status was stronger than it had ever been. That same year, Finland joined the European Monetary and Economic Union, and the country also held the presidency of the European Union Council. In 2002, Finland adopted the euro as its currency.

North Atlantic Treaty Organization (NATO)

After joining the EU (and no doubt prior as well, but post-Soviet Union collapse), Finland contemplated joining NATO. The majority of Finns, however, were comfortable with the status of their country's security. It should be noted that even with Finland's (and Sweden's) membership in the EU, Russia generally continues to refer to both countries as "neutrals." But formally joining NATO is viewed by most political thinkers as being too dramatic of a change in Finland's (and Sweden's) military—as opposed to political—non-alignment. Moscow has often pointed out that formal NATO membership for either country would raise concerns about the balance of power in the Baltic Sea region. (Put another way, they better not.)

The terrorist attacks on the United States on September 1, 2001 shaped the early 2000s of almost every country in the world. EU leaders demonstrated strong support for the U.S., and of course, NATO's response was immediate and aggressive. For the first time ever in its history, the collective defense of Article 5 was invoked. Even though not a member of NATO, Finland joined in the International Security Assistance Force (ISAF) mission that NATO led in Afghanistan. This was not the first time Finland had joined in

NATO operations, the first being during the peacekeeping missions in the Western Balkans in the 1990s.

At the 2014 NATO Summit in Wales, Finland was one of five countries named as eligible for "enhanced opportunities partnership for dialogue and cooperation," or "EOP." The others were: Australia, Georgia, Jordan, and, not surprisingly, Sweden. With this new status, Finland is now even further within the Western community's "circle of trust," and is also able to participate on an equal footing with NATO member states in regard to NATO's working procedures.

ECONOMY

As set out above, even in the midst of Finland's economic depression in the early 1990s, the country wisely invested heavily in research and development. In the 2000s, these investments paid off with the boom of the Finnish ICT (information and communications technology) sector. Nokia in particular became tremendously important to Finland's economy and the country as a whole. In 2000, Nokia produced a whopping 21% of Finnish exports, and from 1998 to 2012, it was the world's largest manufacturer of mobile phones.

Ironically, Finland's technological advances and resulting global interconnectedness are of even more importance to its own country than many others. Recall that Finland is akin to a remote island in the far north, and most winters is ice-bound. Modern information technology has deemed distance and remoteness largely irrelevant for Finns.

Just one of the other high-tech branches where Finland leads in the world is the gaming industry. The Finnish company Rovio created Angry Birds, released in 2009, which became the most downloaded freemium game series of all time as of 2015. And Clash of Clans, one of the top grossing apps on both the App Store and Google Play, was developed by another Finnish company, Supercell.

Finland's startup scene has grown rapidly since the 2000s as well. The now well-known Slush startup conference was organized for the first time in Helsinki in 2008. (And by the way, its name was derived from the amount of icy "slush" there in November, when it is held each year.) That conference now annually attracts almost 20,000 guests from more than a hundred countries.

For decades, the United States has been one of Finland's most important trade partners. Traditionally, Finland exported primarily wood-based products to the U.S., such as paper, pulp, and plywood. In 1960, this sector comprised 84% of Finland's exports to the U.S. But with Finland's membership in the EU, transatlantic economic partnerships were obviously promoted, including an expansion of that with the U.S. For the Finnish economy, this open international trade and investment environment was invaluable. Their exports became much more diversified, as demonstrated above.

Education

In 2000, the OECD (Organization for Economic Cooperation and Development) published its first-ever PISA (Programme for International Student Assessment). This study assesses students at the age of fifteen in mathematics, science, and reading literacy, and of the many participating countries, Finland ranked first in literacy, third in science, and fourth in mathematics. Three years later, Finland was first in reading and science, and second in mathematics. Many education experts from numerous countries began to travel to Finland to try and discover the "secrets" behind Finland's educational success.

As noted above herein, the University of Helsinki is routinely ranked within the top 100 universities in the world, and the top twenty in Europe. Founded in 1640, it is the country's oldest and largest institution of academic education. The University is a founding member of the League of European Research Universities (LERU), an organization that also includes universities such as Oxford and Cambridge. The University of Helsinki's main strength is considered to be scientific research and teaching. Its philosophy is: "All teachers are researchers, and all researchers teach."

It should be noted that in the past decade, Finland has scored extremely well in different international studies that measure how well a society functions. Specifically, in global studies that measure things such as equality, freedom, transparency, innovativeness, and competitiveness, Finland has scored very high. Notably, according to the annual "Fragile States Index," Finland is the "least failed state in the world."

Environment

The Environmental Performance Index (EPI) is prepared by Yale and Columbia Universities, and compares how different countries protect human health and ecosystems. Factors considered include: how the individual countries take care of their water, air, and other resources; how they manage forests, fish, and agriculture; their energy solutions; and their approach to the diversity of nature and climate change.

According to the EPI report, three of the most significant global concerns are lack of clean water, deteriorating air quality, and decreasing fish stocks. As much as half of the world's population suffers from exposure to dangerous respiratory air, and more than 500 million people in the world live without clean water. In 2016, Finland was deemed by the EPI to be the world's cleanest and greenest country, scoring a 90.68.

Finland is one of the most forested countries in the world, with more than 70% of its land being forests. More than 80% of the country's lakes are considered to be either "good" or "excellent" in quality. And according to the WHO (World Health Organization), Finland has the third cleanest air in the world (after Canada and Iceland), and the cleanest air of all the EU countries.

OTHER INTERESTING FINNISH FACTS

1. Finland is often referred to as "the land of thousands of lakes," for a reason: there are 187,888 lakes. The blue color in the Finnish flag is symbolic of all the lakes, and the white is symbolic of the snow.

2. Finnish people enjoy quite unique and interesting sports. Some examples: mobile phone throwing, wife-carrying, and mosquito hunting. Beer in the quantity of the wife's weight is the first-prize in the wife-carrying championship.

3. Believe it or not, there are more *saunas* than *cars* in Finland. Even a Burger King in Helsinki has a sauna.

4. If you have a good income in Finland, beware of speeding! The fines for speeding are based upon the speeder's income! In reality, a millionaire can be fined up to $100,000 for driving too fast.

5. The world's highest consumption of milk, per capita, occurs in Finland.

6. Something that the Finns should really pride themselves on is that education is free for students, even at the university level.

7. In Finland, all of the following amazing events can be experienced: Northern Lights, Midnight Sun, and Polar

Night. There is actually a resort where you watch the Northern Lights from a glass igloo.

8. Finland has a "National Sleepy Head Day" on which the last person in the family to wake up gets thrown into a lake or the sea.

9. Finns do not wear shoes when visiting someone's home. An exception is a big party or celebration of some sort; in that event, guests bring two pairs of shoes—one for outside and one for inside.

10. Finland is ranked as the #1 happiest country in the world. …

For the last several years, the Sustainable Development Solutions Network for the United Nations has ranked countries throughout the world based on "happiness." The six key variables considered that support overall well-being are: freedom, income, trust, social support, healthy life expectancy, and generosity.

On March 20, 2020, the latest UN World Happiness Report named Finland as "the happiest country in the world" for the third year in a row.

* * *

This land, although not my native land,
Will be remembered forever.
And the sea's lightly iced,
Unsalty water.

The sand on the bottom is whiter than chalk,
The air is heady, like wine,
And the rosy body of the pines
Is naked in the sunset hour.

And the sunset itself on such waves of ether
That I just can't comprehend
Whether it is the end of the day, the end of the world,
Or the mystery of mysteries in me again.

(Anna Akhmatova—regarding Finland)

BIBLIOGRAPHY

http://countrystudies.us/finland/20.htm

https://en.wikipedia.org/wiki/Cudgel_War

https://en.wikipedia.org/wiki/European_Free_Trade_Association

https://en.wikipedia.org/wiki/Gustavus_Adolphus_of_Sweden

https://en.wikipedia.org/wiki/Helsinki_Accords

https://en.wikipedia.org/wiki/History_of_Finland

https://en.wikipedia.org/wiki/Independence_of_Finland

https://en.wikipedia.org/wiki/Lapland_War

https://en.wikipedia.org/wiki/Member_states_of_NATO

https://en.wikipedia.org/wiki/Russo-Swedish_War

https://en.wikipedia.org/wiki/Shelling_of_Mainila

https://en.wikipedia.org/wiki/Soviet%E2%80%93Finnish_Non-Aggression_Pact

https://encyclopedia.1914-1918-online.net/article/jager_movement

https://europecentenary.eu/the-finns-in-the-first-world-war/

https://finlandabroad.fi/web/usa/current-affairs/

https://finland.fi/life-society/main-outlines-of-finnish-history/

https://foreignpolicy.com/2016/03/07/how-finland-became-europes-bear-whisperer-russia-putin/

https://harreira.com/viking/which-countries-were-the-vikings-related-to/

http://heninen.net/sopimus/1948_e.htm

https://herfinland.com/facts-on-finland/

https://histdoc.net/history/abo1743.html

https://history.state.gov/departmenthistory/short-history/berlinwall

https://medium.com/war-is-boring/how-a-small-force-of-finnish-ski-troops-fought-off-a-massive-soviet-army-8f7d7a6142c5
http://motherearthtravel.com/history/finland/history-3.htm
https://nationalinterest.org/feature/how-finland-lost-world-war-ii-the-soviets-won-peace-17412
https://nordics.info/en/show/artikel/nordic-council-and-nordic-council-of-ministers/
https://nypost.com/2019/02/10/finland-helped-nazis-murder-jews-during-wwii-report/
https://searchinginhistory.blogspot.com/2014/12/hakkapeliitta-thirty-years-war-and-rise.html
http://users.jyu.fi/~aphamala/pe/2004/cajeugen.htm
https://www.bbc.com/news/world-europe-40731415
https://www.bbc.co.uk/bitesize/guides/z32g87h/revision/3
https://www.britannica.com/event/Battle-of-Poltava
https://www.britannica.com/event/Thirty-Years-War
https://www.britannica.com/place/Finland
https://www.cnbc.com/2015/03/18/who-still-owes-what-for-the-two-world-wars.html
https://www.cnn.com/travel/article/worlds-happiest-country-wellness-2020/index.html
https://www.discoveringfinland.com/about-finland/finnish-history/
https://www.foreigner.fi/opinion/mahmudul-islam/schauman-the-swedish-speaking-finn-who-killed-governor-general-bobrikov/20200304
http://www.gmfus.org/blog/2016/06/29/natos-enhanced-opportunities-partners
https://www.goodreads.com/quotes/tag/finland

https://www.history.com/this-day-in-history/germans-invade-poland
https://www.history.com/topics/cold-war/berlin-wall
https://www.history.com/topics/cold-war/formation-of-nato-and-warsaw-pact
https://www.history.com/topics/reformation/thirty-years-war
https://www.history.com/topics/russia/russian-revolution
https://www.historyextra.com/period/10-strange-historical-facts-about-finland/
https://www.iwm.org.uk/collections/item/object/30019716
https://www.iwm.org.uk/history/a-short-history-of-the-winter-war
https://www.lonelyplanet.com/finland/history
https://www.nato.int/cps/en/natohq/topics_110496.htm
https://www.nato.int/cps/en/natolive/news_89206.htm
https://www.nytimes.com/2008/01/23/world/europe/23iht-spy.4.9448617.html
https://www.osce.org/who/87
https://www.prlib.ru/en/history/619628
https://www.revivingthehelsinkispirit.org/history/1975-helsinki-accords/
https://www.sweden.org.za/russo-sweden-war.html
https://www.swedishnomad.com/facts-about-finland/
https://www.teamgb.com/games/helsinki-1952
https://www.thedockyards.com/actually-finns-among-vikings/
https://www.theguardian.com/world/2018/feb/23/why-finland-allied-itself-with-nazi-germany
https://www.thehistoryreader.com/medieval-history/viking-crusades/

https://www.thevintagenews.com/2018/06/16/molotov-cocktail/
https://www.thoughtco.com/the-treaty-of-versailles-an-overview-1221958
https://www.thoughtco.com/when-did-world-war-2-end-3878473
https://www.topuniversities.com/universities/university-helsinki
https://www.weforum.org/agenda/2017/12/5-amazing-fact-about-finland-on-its-100th-birthday/
http://www.winterwar.com/War'sEnd/moscow_peace_treaty.htm
https://yle.fi/uutiset/osasto/news/attitudes_towards_swedish-speakers_in_finland_hardening_survey_finds/11184342
https://yle.fi/uutiset/osasto/news/civil_war_still_divides_finland_after_100_years_poll_suggests/10025538
https://yle.fi/uutiset/osasto/news/finland_and_the_european_union_its_complicated/10197162

CPSIA information can be obtained
at www.ICGtesting.com
Printed in the USA
LVHW110408200422
716710LV00006B/336